D1174525

Little Green Thumbs

Mary An Van Hage

Illustrated by Bettina Paterson

Photographs by Lucy Tizard

THE MILLBROOK PRESS
Brookfield, Connecticut

Published in the United States in 1996 by

The Millbrook Press
2 Old New Milford Road
Brookfield, Connecticut 06804

First published in Great Britain in 1995 by

Macdonald Young Books
Campus 400
Maylands Avenue
Hemel Hempstead HP2 7EZ

Prepared for Macdonald Young Books by Wendy Knowles
Design and layout by Chris McLeod
Typesetting by Roger Kohn Designs

Printed and bound by Wing King Tong, Hong Kong

Library of Congress Cataloging-in-Publication Data

Van Hage, Mary An.
  Little green thumbs / Mary An Van Hage; illustrated by
Bettina Paterson; photographs by Lucy Tizard.
    p. cm.
  Originally published: Hemel Hempstead: Macdonald
Young Books, 1995.
  Includes bibliographical references and index.
  Summary: Provides ideas and instructions for projects
that involve growing various kinds of plants indoors during
the different seasons.
  ISBN 1-56294-270-0
  1. Gardening–Juvenile literature. 2. Indoor gardening–
Juvenile literature. 3. Nature craft–Juvenile literature. 4.
Handicraft–Juvenile literature. [1. Indoor gardening. 2.
Handicraft.]
  I. Paterson, Bettina, ill. II. Tizard, Lucy, ill. III. Title.
SB457.V35 1996
635.9'86–dc20   95–45497
                                                             CIP
                                                             AC

For your safety

Have fun with the projects in *Little Green Thumbs*—
but remember an adult should always be nearby
when you are gardening. Be careful when using
plastic bags, and whenever you see this symbol

next to a picture or instruction, it means that adult
help is essential at that point—for example, when
carrying the heavy dinosaur garden, punching holes,
or handling fertilizer.

Contents

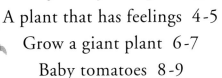

A plant that has feelings

Sow seeds in February or March

This plant is so shy and bashful that if you touch it with your fingertips, the leaves immediately curl up and the branches droop. The leaves also fold up at night, as if they were going to sleep. The sensitive plant's scientific name is *Mimosa pudica*, and it is fun to grow this plant from seed.

Don't close the leaves too often or too roughly

At nighttime it goes to "sleep"

You will need

Mimosa pudica seeds—from garden centers in early spring

Seed tray, foil tray, or margarine tub with holes punched in bottom for drainage

Saucer or tray—for seed trays to stand on

Seed-starting soil mix

Watering can with fine spray or rinsed out pump-action sprayer

For transplanting when seedlings are established:

Plant pots with saucers

Houseplant potting soil

Spoon

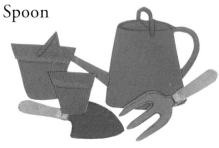

What to do

1 **In February or March**

Wash your container or seed tray. Fill it with seed-starting mix to just below the rim. Gently pack down the soil. Sprinkle a few seeds over it, leaving a space between each seed.

2 **Cover seeds gently with a thin layer of soil**

Water gently, using watering can. The soil should be just moist. Do not drown the seeds or wash them away!

4

Seed growth or germination

1 **Place your seed tray in a warm spot**

A warm windowsill or near a radiator at 68°F (20°C) is ideal. If the tray is on a windowsill, take it off at night, and in cold weather and place in a warmer spot inside the room. Seeds need air and moisture as well as warmth to germinate.

They will not need light until they start to grow. Water when the soil starts to dry out. Do not water if the soil is still moist, or it will become soggy and drown your seeds! Never let the soil dry out completely.

2 **You seeds will germinate in 2-4 weeks**

Move the tray to a windowsill as soon as the seedlings appear. They now need plenty of light to grow. Take them off the windowsill on cold nights. Continue watering carefully as soon as the soil starts to dry, but do not make it soggy. Plants grow toward the light. Turn your tray every 1or 2 days so the seedlings grow upright.

When the seedlings are 2 inches (5 centimeters) high transfer each tiny plant to its own pot

1 **Fill the pot's base with houseplant potting soil**

Gently ease each tiny plant out of the seed tray. Be careful not to damage roots or stems. Use a spoon to help.

2 **Holding the plant gently by its lower leaves, set it on the soil**

Do not hold or squeeze the stem. Fill the pot with more soil to just below the rim. Press down gently and water lightly to help settle the soil. Keep it in a warm, light spot until new growth appears.

Looking after your sensitive plant

Keep it in a brightly lit spot, with some sun, at ordinary room temperature. Let the soil dry out a little between waterings. Don't close the leaves too often. You may damage them.

Grow a giant plant

A giant sunflower grows very quickly into a huge plant from a single seed, just like Jack's beanstalk! Start off by growing the seeds in little pots indoors to give you tiny sunflower plants. Each one can then be planted in a sunny spot in the garden to grow into a giant sunflower by July. If you have grown several tiny sunflower plants, you could sell some at your school bazaar or give some away to your friends.

Scientists call the sunflower Helianthus annus, *and it is a hardy annual. This means that it will last for a year and can live outside even during frosty weather.*

Sow seeds in March

You will need

2 or 3 sunflower seeds—the giant variety *Helianthus annus*

Some yogurt tubs with holes punched in the bottom

Seed starting mix

A pencil

For later on

A strong, tall stake or stick

Some string

What to do

1 Sow your seeds in April

Fill your pots about ³/4 full of seed-starting mix. Make a hole about 1 inch (2.5 centimeters) deep with a pencil, and place one seed in the hole. Cover with more compost and water well.

2 Leave pots on a cool, bright windowsill at about 61°F (16°C)

By early May your seeds will have grown into tiny plants. Check their soil each day and add more water if it feels dry. Do not make it soggy!

3 Let the plants slowly get used to being outside

Start by putting them outside on mild days, then mild nights. After a week, your sunflowers should be used to being outside and can be planted in a sunny spot.

4 Water well in dry weather

This means every day or every other day, even on cloudy days and especially when it is windy. If you give little pots of tiny sunflower plants to your friends, remember to tell them to plant them in a sunny spot and water well.

5 Your plant will grow to 3-10 feet (1-3 meters) tall

By July it will grow a huge yellow sunflower at the top of the stalk. Your sunflower is now so tall and heavy you may need to tie it to a strong, tall stake or fence to help it stay upright.

6 After your sunflower has finished flowering...

You will see the flower head has made masses of seeds. Leave these for the birds to eat, or you can cut off the flower head, store it in a cool, dry place for a few weeks and harvest your own crop of seeds.

You cannot eat these seeds. The part you can eat is inside the strong outer husk. But if you store the seeds in a cool, dry place you can use them to feed the birds in winter, or save them for planting again next April.

Baby tomatoes

A dwarf tomato variety such as "Tiny Tim" produces delicious mini tomatoes, has a small and bushy shape, and is perfect for growing in a pot or tub. You can grow the seedlings in little pots on the windowsill, and then in early summer when the weather is warmer, place them in a very sunny spot outside on a balcony, windowsill, or in a sheltered corner of the garden. By July or August you will be eating your own home-grown juicy tomatoes!

Plant in March or April

You will need

Dwarf variety of tomato seed – pick out the biggest seeds to use

Seed-starting mix – let it warm up a little before using by keeping indoors

Small peat pots to sow seeds in

Seed tray to stand peat pots in

Drip tray or large plate to stand pots and seed tray on

Watering can with fine spray

For later on

Potting soil

Liquid tomato fertilizer

One $2^{1}/_{2}$ - 4-inch (7-10-centimeter) flower pot for each tomato plant

One $6^{1}/_{2}$ - $7^{1}/_{2}$-inch (17-20-centimeter) flower pot for each tomato plant

What to do

1 Sow your seeds in March or April indoors

Fill peat pots almost to the top with seed-starting mix. Place a seed in each and cover with a very thin layer of soil. Pat this down gently and water lightly with tepid water, using a fine spray. Do not make it soggy!

2 Place the little pots in a seed tray

Put a drip tray under the seed tray. Leave in a warm spot, about 64°F (18°C) to germinate. Tiny seedlings should start to show after about a week.

3 As soon as the tiny seedlings start to show...

Move the pots to your sunniest windowsill. Turn the tray every day to prevent the seedlings from leaning toward the light and growing crooked. Take tray off sill at night and bring into the warm room.

Looking after your tomato plants

1 Fertilizing

Start feeding your plants when they produce tiny shoots, like little arms, called flower trusses. Feed them once a week with liquid tomato fertilizer. Dilute it, then water it in. The trusses will become flowers first, then tomatoes.

2 Wait for warm weather, then start to "harden off" your plants

Begin in May or June by standing them outside in a very sunny, sheltered spot during the warm part of the day and bringing them in at night. Leave them out for longer each day, provided the weather is warm, until they are outside all the time. Water now whenever the soil begins to dry out. In July or August your tomatoes will be ready.

Your tomato plant does not need much space, but it will always grow best in the sunniest spot you can find.

4 Watering your seedlings

From now on, water with tepid water whenever the soil feels dry. When you see roots coming out of the bottom of the pots, put a little soil between each pot to prevent the tiny root tips from drying out.

5 Repot when 2½-4 inches (7-10 centimeters) tall

Fill base of 2½-4-inch (7-10-centimeter) plant pot with potting soil. Drop peat pot into it and fill in all around with soil, patting down gently. Water whenever the soil feels dry, keeping it moist but not soggy. Keep turning the pots every day on your sunny windowsill.

6 Repot again when 5½ inches (15 centimeters) tall

Gently remove plant, complete with peat pot and any soil clinging to its roots, from its pot. Repot your plant into a 6½-7½-inch (17-20-centimeter) plant pot as before.

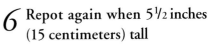

Don't be a prize pumpkin ... grow one instead!

Plant in April or May

Ready for Halloween

Did you know that pumpkins can grow to nearly 200 pounds (90 kilograms)? Or that you could grow four or five pumpkins from just one seed? You will need a sunny, sheltered spot in the garden to plant your seedlings, or you can grow them in a tub on a balcony or patio. But wherever you grow your pumpkins you you need to allow about 6 feet (1.8 meters) all around it—they take up a large space!

Pumpkins love warmth and sunshine, so the ideal growing spot is a sunny place, out of the wind.

What to do

1 **Growing your seedlings**

In April or May fill a flower pot with seed-starting mix. Push in one seed, upright, 1 inch (2.5 centimeters) below the surface. Water and place on a warm windowsill. Keep the soil moist but not soggy. Wait for the shoot to grow to 4 inches (10 centimeters) and to produce 2 or 3 leaves before taking it out of its pot and transplanting it.

2 **In May or June take the seedling out of its pot**

Place stones in the bottom of your tub, and fill with soil mixed with manure. Or fill the hole in the garden with soil and manure. Place the seedling on top. Mound the soil up around it, then water well.

3 **Place the tub in a warm, sunny, sheltered spot**

The seedling now needs lots of warmth and sunshine. It must be sheltered from the wind. Be patient and let it grow. Don't let it dry out.

You will need

Pumpkin seeds

Small plant pot and saucer or
yogurt tub with holes punched in
the bottom

Seed-starting mix

Watering can with fine spray

Some liquid plant fertilizer

An old bucket or tub—or any
container 9¹/₂ inches (25
centimeters) in size or larger,
with holes drilled for drainage

Stones or gravel for drainage
in your container

Or, a hole in the garden, 24
inches (60 centimeters) wide and
18 inches (45 centimeters) deep

Composted manure,
if you can get it

*Your pumpkins will be ready by
September. You could eat them
baked as pumpkin pie, or make
a jack o' lantern for Halloween.*

4 **Your plant will grow runners**

The runners will grow to about
4-5 feet (120-150 centimeters)
all around. Pumpkin fruits will
form along these. Try to provide
lots of space around your plant
(ideally 6 feet [180 centimeters])
and keep training the runners
around and around in that space.

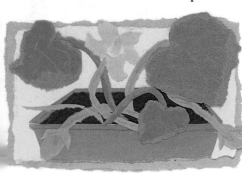

5 **Feeding and watering**

Continue to water well. As soon
as the fruits start forming, feed
once a week with liquid plant
fertilizer, which you dilute
and water in. You can also
fertilize the plant through
the leaves, by moistening them
with the diluted
mixture. Use the
fine spray on your
watering can.
When your
pumpkin fruits
start growing
bigger, fertilize
twice a week.

6 **Pamper your pumpkins!**

Never let the soil dry out.
Always water with tepid water.
Support the runners on bricks
so they won't be damaged by
hanging down. If it's windy,
make a little shelter.

11

Eggstraordinary Easter succulents

Succulents are small plants with fat stems and leaves for storing water, so they can live on much less water than other plants. Grow small succulents inside eggshells, and stand them inside a painted egg carton on your sunniest windowsill. It is easy to take cuttings from succulents in the spring and summer so you can have fun growing lots of new plants in time for Easter!

You will need

Cardboard carton of large-sized eggs

Small succulent plants– available from garden centers

A couple of handfuls of cactus soil or some potting soil with sand mixed in

Plant sprayer

Scissors

Poster paints and brush

Spring flowers and Easter decorations

Take cuttings several weeks before Easter

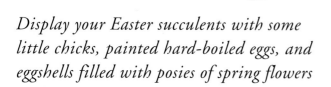

Display your Easter succulents with some little chicks, painted hard-boiled eggs, and eggshells filled with posies of spring flowers

What to do

1 Several weeks before Easter, prepare your succulent containers

Paint your egg carton in bright colors. Slice the tops off your eggs and wash the shells out. Place soil in the eggshells, filling each shell almost to the top.

2 Take stem cuttings from succulents with an upright, tree-like shape, like Sedum

Cut 2 or 3 pieces of stem from the plant, each piece about 2-2½ inches (5-7 centimeters) long, with lots of leaves. Remove the lower leaves, leaving pieces of bare stem about ¾ inch (2 centimeters) long. Push these into the soil in the eggshell so the cuttings stand upright. Mist with the sprayer to moisten the soil.

3 Take whole leaf cuttings from succulents with large or pointed leaves, like Crassula

Break off a leaf near the base of the plant. Push the leaf end into the soil in the eggshell so that the cutting stands upright. Plant 2 or 3 cuttings in each eggshell. Mist with the sprayer to moisten the soil.

4 Instant plants using ready-grown succulents

Take each ready-grown succulent out of its pot. Fill the base of the eggshell with soil. Place the plant inside the eggshell. Fill in gently with more soil. Mist with the sprayer to moisten the soil.

Your cuttings will take several weeks to take root

Looking after your succulents

1 Place your egg carton in a light, warm place

A sunny windowsill is ideal. Let the soil dry out between waterings, then moisten again carefully, using a sprayer or tiny watering can. Do not overwater—remember there is nowhere for the water to go! In winter succulents like to be kept dry, so water less often.

2 When the plants grow bigger ...

Repot them into small pots in the spring. In summer, succulents like a warm, light place. In winter, they like a cool, light spot.

Mr. and Mrs. Grass and family

Plant any time in spring or summer

You can create your own family of silly "grass people." They're fun to make and decorate, and in a short time they will amaze you with their heads of bright-green hair.

Your grass person's hair may need a trim from time to time

You will need

For one grown-up grass person

One and a half handfuls of grass seed

A pair of nylon stockings (1 leg per grass person)

Scissors

18-ounce (1/2-liter) jug full of sawdust—available from pet shops

Cotton thread—same color as stockings, or a very small rubber band

Waterproof container to hold each grass person—for example, a plastic tub or a glass, about 2-3 inches (6-7 centimeters) in diameter

Felt and buttons or sequins and scraps of material or ribbon

Non-toxic waterproof craft glue

For a child-sized grass person

1 nylon sock (child-size)

1 cup (1/4 liter) of sawdust

1 handful of grass seed

Same material as for a grown-up grass person

What to do

1 Make stocking tube

Cut feet off stockings, leaving a piece of leg 7-10 inches (20-25 centimeters) long. Tie a knot at one end of this. Trim any material above knot. Turn stocking inside out so knot is on the inside.

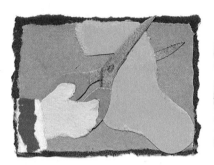

2 Pour grass seeds into the tube

Make sure the seeds are in the middle of the tube. This will be the top of the head, from which the green grass hair will grow. Pour in about a handful of the sawdust (less for a child-sized person). Press down firmly.

3 Now for the nose

Take a clump of sawdust between fingers and thumb and push it outward from inside the stocking. Take hold of it from the outside with your other hand to form the nose. Tie up the nose with the thread or rubber band. Trim any loose threads.

4 Pour rest of the sawdust into the tube

Press the sawdust down so it is tightly packed. Pull stocking tight around sawdust. Twist the stocking around once and tie in a tight knot. Trim the stocking above the knot.

5 Making the head

Pat and squeeze the knotted sawdust tube into a round head shape. Turn upside down so the grass seeds lie on the top of the head, ready to sprout as hair.

6 Decorating the face

Add eyebrows, ears, or even a moustache and some clothes!

With light, warmth, and moisture your grass family's hair will grow!

Place them on a light, sunny windowsill

Stand them in containers on a drip tray. Water well. Pour water over the heads and fill the containers with water. Do not let the seeds and sawdust dry out. After the grass hair has grown, continue to water well. Keep the water level in the containers up to the top. The sawdust will soak up water like a sponge, helping to keep the hair fresh and green.

Yum yum, gobble gobble, flies for a snack!

How to look after a Venus flytrap Plant

This is an insect-eating plant called the Venus flytrap. The Venus flytrap uses its trap-like leaves to catch its own dinner! Its scientific name is *Dionaea muscipula,* and it originally comes from the swamp lands of North Carolina. You can have fun growing one at home.

Late spring or summer

You will need

Small or medium-sized Venus flytrap—the best time to get one from a garden center is late spring or summer

Cover for your plant in winter—large glass or plastic bag

For repotting in spring

Small pot

Special potting mix from a garden center or some multi-purpose potting soil with a handful of sphagnum moss mixed in.

What to do—in summer

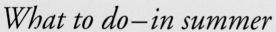

1 **Place your flytrap in a bright spot indoors**

Flytraps like average warmth. Keep yours out of reach of bright sun coming through the glass. This can scorch it.

2 **In warm weather**

Flytraps don't like to be too hot. Put yours in a sunny spot out in the fresh air. Then the sun's rays won't feel so hot and it can catch more food!

3 **Catch some rainwater**

Use this to water your plant. Keep your flytrap moist. Do not let it dry out, but do not overwater so that it gets soggy.

When an insect lands on the trap, it activates tiny hairs that work like triggers to shut the trap. It takes several days for the closed trap to digest the insect and open again. The warmer the weather, the quicker the traps will close. Do not close the traps by force. This will weaken them.

You can feed small dead insects into the traps in summertime

Brrr–It's winter, your flytrap is freezing

4 **Cover your flytrap with a glass jar**

This keeps the air around it humid and warm. Take the cover off occasionally to let in air and get rid of condensation.

5 **Place on a bright windowsill**

Never let the soil get cold and soggy. Let the surface of the soil dry out between waterings. Keep at room temperature.

6 **Don't worry if the plant dies back**

It starts to grow again in the spring. In winter the flytrap plant is resting. In spring take the plant out of its pot and replant using fresh soil.

Plants from pits—grow an orange inside an orange!

or a lemon inside a grapefruit

Citrus fruits, like oranges, lemons, tangerines, limes, and grapefruits, all contain pits or seeds that you can plant in little pots of soil in spring. When the seedlings appear, it is fun to plant them inside an empty orange or grapefruit rind, and let them grow for a while on a sunny windowsill before potting them.

You will need

Citrus fruit pits—soak them in water for 2 days before using

Small plant pot and saucer to stand it on

Potting soil

Pencil

Plastic bag and twist-tie

2 or 3 citrus fruits cut in half

Knitting needle

Plant in spring or early summer

Your citrus tree could last for years, but won't make any fruit unless it grows to about 6 feet (1.8 meters) tall!

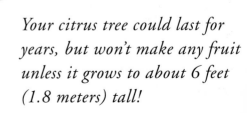

18

What to do

1 **In spring, plant your pits**

Fill a plant pot with soil. Use a pencil to make a hole about 3/4 inch (2 centimeters) deep. Plant 2 or 3 pits, then water lightly, so soil is just moist.

2 **Place pot inside plastic bag**

Tie the top and leave in a warm, dark place to germinate (about 70°F [21°C]). This could take 3-4 weeks. If drops of water appear on the inside of the bag, just shake or flick the bag so the drops run down.

3 **As soon as the shoots appear...**

Remove the plastic bag and place the pot in a light, warm spot. Water when the soil feels dry. Keep it just moist and not too wet.

4 **When the seedlings are 2-3 inches (5-6 centimeters) long...**

Scoop out the insides of your citrus halves. Make lots of holes in the rind, from the inside, with your knitting needle. Put a little soil in the base.

5 **Plant the seedlings**

Remove seedlings from their pot. Place one in the center of each rind. Fill in all around with soil—try not to damage the roots. Pack down gently and add a little water to settle the soil. From now on, water whenever the soil feels dry.

Growing a citrus tree

1 **When the seedlings are 4 inches (10 centimeters) tall, or if any green mold starts to form**

Plant each into its own pot of soil. Your citrus will grow quickly and develop a good root system. In spring and summer, water it well and feed every 3-4 weeks with plant food.

2 **You can put it outside in summer**

Citrus love sunshine and fresh air. But remember to bring the plants indoors again before the cold weather comes. In winter water much less and keep it in a light, cool spot. Next spring, if it is doing well, you can put your tree into a bigger pot with fresh soil.

Christmas tulips

Bright and colorful tulips usually bloom outdoors in spring, but if you plant them in late summer or early autumn, you can make them flower indoors in time for Christmas. Choose early-flowering deep-red dwarf tulips, and when they bloom, decorate them to make a beautiful Christmas display.

Plant in August or early September

Little Red Riding Hood is a good red tulip to grow in little pots because it is not too tall

1 **Late August or early September**

Place some potting soil in your pots. Position the bulbs upright on the soil so they are close, but not touching.

2 **Cover bulbs with soil**

Make sure the soil does not go right to the top of the pots or they will overflow when you water! Water well.

3 **Place pots in a black plastic bag**

Leave in a cold, dark place—a shed or cellar, or even the refrigerator, for 10-12 weeks. Check soil now and then. If dry, add water, but do not make it soggy.

4 **When shoots are 2 inches (5 centimeters) high**

Put the bulbs on a cool, bright windowsill for 7-10 days. Water carefully only if the soil feels dry. The shoots will soon be turning green.

5 **When shoots are 4 inches (10 centimeters) high**

Move to a warm, light spot. Wait 2-3 weeks for your tulips to flower in time for Christmas. If you find your tulips are coming out too quickly, move them to a cooler spot.

6 **Looking after your tulips**

Turn the pots every 2-3 days so each side gets an equal amount of light, otherwise the tulips will grow lop-sided. Keep pots away from drafts, fires, or radiators.

Decorating your pots

Have fun making a colorful Christmas display. Choose from:

Pinecones or holly, left plain or painted gold, red, white, or silver.

Festive ribbon—red, white, gold, or silver.

Homemade decorations, like felt Christmas trees decorated with beads and gold thread.

Group several different-sized pots together. Try to keep to the same colors.

Hyacinth star basket

Plant from early- to mid-September

Brighten up the dark days of winter with sweet-smelling silvery-pink hyacinth bulbs. Watch the roots growing in a glass jar filled with water, or make your own hyacinth star basket.

You will need

Potting soil mix

Sphagnum moss

Prepared or forced hyacinth bulbs. These can make your skin feel itchy, so wear gloves before touching them and wash your hands afterward

Basket—at least 4 inches (10 centimeters) deep, and a sheet of plastic to line it

Black plastic bag

Star-shaped stencils, heavy colored paper, ribbon, beads, buttons, and glitter

Scissors and non-toxic craft glue

Glass bulb jar or narrow vase

Silver and pink decorations look pretty with pale-pink hyacinths

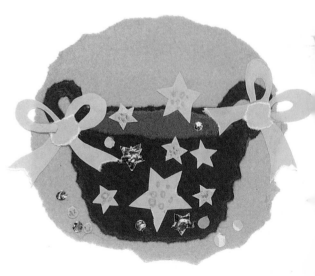

Have fun decorating your basket

Put sphagnum moss around the bulbs to cover the soil. Tie on pretty ribbons and bows. Cut out star shapes, paint them, and glue on beads or buttons. Shake a little glitter over the stars to make them twinkle, and attach them to your basket with glue.

22

What to do

1 Early- or mid- September

Line your basket with plastic and put some potting soil in it. Place your bulbs on the soil with the "noses" up, so that they are close but not touching.

2 **Almost cover the bulbs with soil**

Leave just the "noses" sticking out. Make sure the soil doesn't go right to the top of the basket, or it will overflow when you water. Water enough to make the soil moist but not soggy.

3 **Keep your bulbs cold and dark**

Wrap the basket in a black bag and place it in a cold, dark, place like a garage, shed, or refrigerator for 10-12 weeks. Check the soil every week and water if it is dry.

4 **When the shoots are about 2 inches (5 centimeters) high**

Take the basket out of the bag and put it in a cool, shady place indoors.

5 **A week or so later, when the shoots are about 4 inches (10 centimeters) high...**

Move the basket to a warm, bright windowsill away from drafts or radiators. Keep watering, but don't let the soil get soggy!

6 **Turn your basket around every 2-3 days...**

Otherwise your bulbs will grow lop-sided. If you find your hyacinths are coming out too quickly, move them to a cooler spot. This will make the flowers last longer.

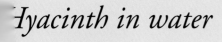

Hyacinth in water

1 Fill your bulb jar with water. Sit the bulb on the top, so it almost, but not quite, touches the water. Put it in a cold, dark place. Check the water level once a week and keep it filled up.

2 When the roots are about 4 inches (10 centimeters) long and there is a yellow shoot on top, take your bulb jar out of the dark. Keep it in semi-darkness for 2 days. This helps to get the shoot used to the light gradually.

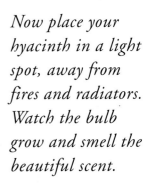

Now place your hyacinth in a light spot, away from fires and radiators. Watch the bulb grow and smell the beautiful scent.

Crocus on shells and pebbles

Plant September or early October

Colorful crocuses usually flower outdoors in early spring, but you can grow them on your windowsill much earlier, using just a saucer or a shallow container of water and some pebbles or shells.

Crocus bulbs

Small pebbles, gravel or seashells

Shallow, leak-proof containers—such as saucers, sardine tins, old ashtrays, or large shells

Large flower pots or dishes

Strong, non-toxic craft glue

Pastel poster paints and brush

Scissors

Heavy paper, ribbon, shells, and dried seaweed for decorating your containers

Blue, purple, and white crocuses are easier to grow indoors than yellow ones

What to do

1 In September or early October

Wash the pebbles and shells. Place them in your containers. Pour in a little water so that it nearly reaches to the top of the pebbles and shells.

2 Set the bulbs on the shells

Their "noses" should be pointing up. Leave a small space between each bulb. Make sure the water level is below the bulbs so that they are not sitting in water. The bulbs' roots will sense water is near, and reach out toward it.

3 Leave the bulbs in a cold, dark cellar or shed, or in the refrigerator

Cover them with an upturned flower pot to make it extra dark and to keep mice away! The darkness and cold make the crocuses think winter has arrived, so they make roots, ready for spring. The water may need refilling so it stays just below the bulbs.

4 After 8-10 weeks …when the shoots are about 2 inches (5 centimeters) high…

Move your containers to a light windowsill, away from fire, radiators, or the stove. Even if it is snowing outside the crocuses now think it is spring, and will soon bloom.

5 Making the flowers last longer

Keep them in a cool spot. Refill with water if necessary.

6 After flowering

Don't throw away your bulbs. Plant them outside in a sunny, sheltered spot for more blooms next year.

The train now arriving on platform 2

Plant any time

Make a watercress train, with each truck carrying its cargo of sprouting green watercress seeds. They taste delicious in your sandwiches! Watercress seeds can be sown any time of year and are ready to eat by the end of a week.

What to do

1 Make your train cars

Turn cartons on their sides. Cut off the tops to make cars. Paint the cars in bright colors. Keep one carton for the engine.

2 Make an engine and wheels

Draw your train and wheel shapes. Cut them out and paint them. When dry, glue the engine and wheels to the cars to make a train.

3 Sow watercress seeds

Wet some cotton balls. Place them in each car so that the car is half full. Sprinkle the seeds on top in a thin layer.

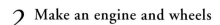

When your train is empty,
you can always sow some
more seeds in the cars

Leave the seeds to germinate

Place the cars in a warm, dark spot. After 2 or 3 days your seeds should start to sprout.

As soon as the seeds sprout

Put the cars in a light place. Spray the cotton lightly to make sure it stays damp. Try not to spray the paint.

When your watercress is about 2 inches (5 centimeters) high...

It will be ready to eat! Snip the seedlings with scissors and sprinkle on your sandwiches. Delicious!

When dinosaurs roamed the earth

Two hundred million years ago, dinosaurs lived on earth. Despite their huge size, many of them were herbivores, which meant they ate only plants. Scientists also believe they ate stones to help with their digestion! Now you can create your own prehistoric landscape, complete with dinosaurs, stones, and plants, in a fish tank.

Plant any time

Oblong glass container

Houseplant potting soil

Washed gravel or pebbles

A few handfuls of charcoal for aquariums

Small rocks, pebbles, pieces of bark, or driftwood to decorate

2 or 3 larger rocks or stones for your boulders

Plant sprayer

Model dinosaurs—the same size as some of your taller plants

6 or 7 small houseplants—those sold in 3 1/2 inch (9 centimeter) pots or the tinier bottle garden plants

Choose from:

Tall, tree-shaped plants, like parlor palm or any of the palms; *Dracaena*; umbrella tree.

Bushy plants, like polka-dot plant; Boston fern or any of the ferns; *Peperomia*.

Small-leaved plants to cover the ground, like baby's tears; club moss; creeping fig.

A *Lithops* or two would be fun—they are small succulent plants also called living stones.

What to do

1 Making your prehistoric landscape

Place a layer of pebbles or gravel ¾ inch (18 millimeters) thick on the tank base. Cover with a thinner layer of charcoal and put soil on top, 2-3 inches (5-7 centimeters) deep. Shape hills and valleys and position your boulders.

2 Planting

Water your plants well and make small holes in the soil for them. Ease them out of their pots and put them in the holes. Put taller plants at the back and let the trailing plants tumble over your boulders. Fill in the gaps with the bushy plants. Pack the soil around each plant.

3 Make your landscape look wild and rough

Put in more rocks, stones, and pieces of bark. Water it very lightly, just enough to make the soil moist. Clean the tank walls with a damp cloth. Put in your dinosaurs!

Looking after your dinosaur landscape

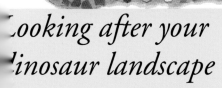

1 Put it in a warm room with lots of natural light

Keep it out of direct sunlight. In summer, hot rays of sunlight through glass can burn plants. Never put it near a south-facing window. Spray the leaves regularly with tepid water to make the air moist.

2 Watering your landscape

Only water when the soil is slightly dry. Let it dry between waterings. Use just enough water to moisten the soil. Too much water in your tank will turn the soil soggy and rot and kill your plants.

3 Trimming

Cut back long or straggly plants with a small pair of sharp scissors.

"Honey, I shrunk the garden!"

Start anytime

Try making your own indoor miniature garden with tiny indoor bottle garden plants.

You will need

Basket of gardening tools

Seed tray or any similar-shaped container

Washed gravel or pebbles—enough to spread a layer over the base of your container

2 or 3 handfuls of charcoal for aquariums

Houseplant potting soil

A little grass seed, moss, or turf for a lawn

Pebbles or small stones for a path

Dried or artificial flowers

Pinecones, painted green, for bushes

Mirror or shallow foil container for a pond

Little house, people or animal figures

Place your garden in a light spot out of harsh summer sun. Keep the soil just moist. Only water when the soil is slightly dry.

A few tiny indoor plants

Choose from: Tree-shapes, like palms or fern bush-shapes, like club moss or *Peperomia* or *Croton*; low-growing, trailing plants with small leaves, like ivy or creeping fig; colorful-leaved plants, like polka-dot plant, mother of thousands, or wandering Jew.